What's So Great About Me?
I'm Nothing. Just a Zombie!

Written and Illustrated
By

Edward Kent

Copyright 2015 by Lobster Love LLC
All Rights Reserved

ISBN 13 - 978-1508693321
ISBN 10 - 1508693323

Library of Congress Control Number: 2015904181

CreateSpace Independent Publishing Platform, North Charleston, SC

This book is dedicated to all the individuals out there that are truly one of a kind. The world would be extremely dull if we were all the same!

Ed's a zombie, it's plain to see,

But he's a bit different than you or me.

He's not so fast as to win a race,

It's not too often he gets first place.

His arm is bones and his face is pale,

Ed's legs are as thin as a coffin nail.

Ed wishes he was fast and strong,

Everything about him he feels is wrong.

Why can't he be more like everyone else?

He gets sad sometimes, and his heart just melts.

Ed wants to be fast and not so gray,

A fleshy arm for work and play.

Ed's not usually picked first in gym,

and he never hears "I want HIM!"

His clothes aren't "cool" like the other kids' are,

A torn shirt and shorts won't get him far.

"I want to be like the living boys and girls,

No bones sticking out, cool clothes, and maybe some curls."

"I'm not much good at too many sports or gym,

And it's hard for me on pool days, because I can't swim."

Ed would go home and lay in his bed,

thinking to himself, "Why do I have to be undead?"

Then one day at school, while Ed was feeling down,

the gym teacher asked him, "Why the long frown?"

Ed explained to him his problem, and why he was sad,

the teacher exclaimed, "Why that's not so bad!"

"Everyone is special, and comes with their own cool traits,

so being a little different is a good thing, for goodness sakes!"

"You see, you're a zombie, Ed, that's who you were meant to be,

Just like being born a gym teacher, that is me."

"If we were all the same, what fun would that be?

It's important to be who we are, and you're as special as you can be."

"You see John sitting over there next to Laurie? He can't draw very well, but he sure knows how to write a good story!"

"And Alexis is really good at soccer, but can't remember the combination to her locker."

He explained that all people have different hair, or need to wear glasses,

and some kids need to be placed in special classes.

For every thing you think is wrong with you,

There's at least a dozen things you're good at too.

Ed sat there and thought about all he had said,

He realized that maybe it wasn't so bad being a zombie named Ed.

Getting hit by a baseball caused him no pain,

And he never caught cold standing out in the rain.

The more Ed thought about it, the better he understood.

Perhaps being a zombie was actually pretty good!

Everyone is special, with their own strengths and faults,

Everybody has problems, no matter how big or how small.

"We are all different and special and that is okay."

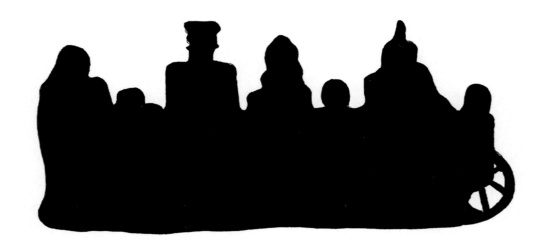

"The world would be boring if that weren't the way."

"I like who I am, alive or undead,"

"There's only one me, only one Zombie Ed!"

About the Author

Edward Kent lives in the quiet town of West Seneca, New York, located 15 minutes from downtown Buffalo, with his wife Dannielle, and their three children: Cordelia, Keifer, and Brody.

He grew up in a small town off Lake Ontario, and after high school, attended Niagara University where he received a BA, majoring in Theatre.

After receiving his Masters in Education, he taught second grade in Virginia Beach, Virginia for two years before relocating back to Western New York.

Time was spent teaching middle school, as well as working as a trainer for a major dialysis company, before beginning his new career as an author.

The author is a member of the Society of Children's Book Writers & Illustrators.

Visit the author at www.ZombieEdUndead.com

Look for these other Zombie Ed titles:

All titles available through the author's website at www.ZombieEdUndead.com